STARK LIBRARY JUL -- 2020

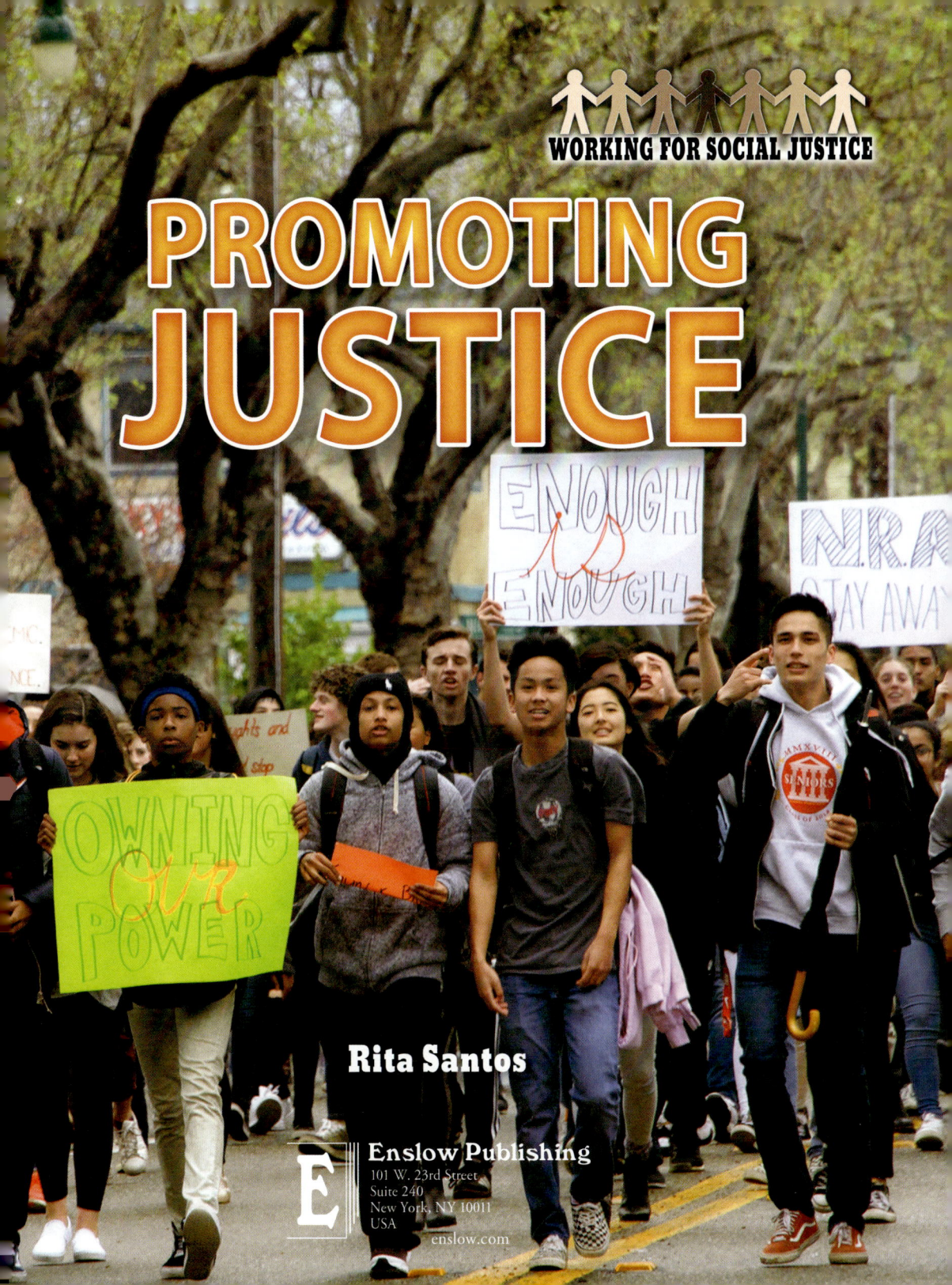

Published in 2020 by Enslow Publishing, LLC.
101 W. 23rd Street, Suite 240, New York, NY 10011

Copyright © 2020 by Enslow Publishing, LLC.

All rights reserved.

No part of this book may be reproduced by any means without the written permission of the publisher.

Library of Congress Cataloging-in-Publication Data

Names: Santos, Rita, author.
Title: Promoting justice / Rita Santos.
Description: New York : Enslow Publishing, 2020. | Series: Working for social justice | Includes bibliographical references and index. | Audience: Grades 3-6.
Identifiers: LCCN 2018048406| ISBN 9781978507869 (library bound) | ISBN 9781978507982 (pbk.) | ISBN 9781978507999 (6 pack)
Subjects: LCSH: Social justice—Juvenile literature. | Equality—Juvenile literature.
Classification: LCC HM671 .S276 2020 | DDC 303.3/72—dc23
LC record available at https://lccn.loc.gov/2018048406

Printed in the United States of America

To Our Readers: We have done our best to make sure all website addresses in this book were active and appropriate when we went to press. However, the author and the publisher have no control over and assume no liability for the material available on those websites or on any websites they may link to. Any comments or suggestions can be sent by email to customerservice@enslow.com.

Photo Credits: Cover, p. 1 Sheila Fitzgerald/Shutterstock.com; p. 5 © iStockphoto.com/FatCamera; p. 6 mikeledray/Shutterstock.com; p. 9 triocean/Shutterstock.com; p. 11 Jacob Lund/Shutterstock.com; p. 12 Joseph Sohm/Shutterstock.com; p. 15 Bandersnatch/Shutterstock.com; p. 17 oneword/Shutterstock.com; p. 19 M-SUR/Shutterstock.com; p. 20 a katz/Shutterstock.com; p. 22 © iStockphoto.com/Image Source; p. 25 Bryan R. Smith/AFP/Getty Images; p. 26 Photo 12/Universal Images Group/Getty Images; p. 28 stock_photo_world/Shutterstock.com; cover graphics Stankovic/Shutterstock.com.

CONTENTS

Introduction **4**

CHAPTER ONE
What Is Justice? **8**

CHAPTER TWO
Who Gets Justice? **14**

CHAPTER THREE
Battling the Unconscious **19**

CHAPTER FOUR
Working Toward Justice for All **24**

Words to Know **30**

Learn More **31**

Index **32**

Introduction

Everyone's had an unfair experience. Maybe someone cut you in line. Or you missed out on a snack because someone else took more than their share. These kinds of things feel unfair because they break the rules. When the government makes a rule it's called a law. When we talk about what's fair or unfair, we're talking about the concept of **justice**.

When you've felt something was unfair you probably wanted someone to step in and correct the situation. In the United States, the judicial branch of the government enforces laws and punishes those who break them. But justice isn't just about punishment. Justice can also mean preventing unfairness from happening in the first place. Many people believe justice is also about ensuring that people are treated fairly and equally.

You may have heard the saying "justice is blind." This means that everyone, no matter who they are, should be treated the same in the eyes of the law. But our police officers, our judges, and jury members are all just people, and people make mistakes. While we do our best to make sure everyone is treated fairly,

The unfair experiences we've had can teach us about justice and the importance of fairness.

Some black citizens have been unfairly targeted or profiled by police officers because of bias.

fairly, some people simply are not. People of color and LGBTQ people are often the targets of others' unconscious biases.

People don't always agree about what's fair. As society changes, our views of what is just or unjust may also change. Our legal system acts as a guide for what behavior is unfair but it doesn't cover everything. The concept of justice extends beyond the courtroom. Just because something is legal doesn't mean it's fair.

In comic books, superheroes are the defenders of justice. In the real world, anyone can be a superhero. We can all help to right injustices in our communities, too. Understanding justice allows us to spot things in our communities and the world that are unfair. When we come together to work for a more just society the world becomes a fairer and nicer place for everybody.

one

What Is Justice?

Most superheroes fight for justice, but what does that mean? In comic books it means that the bad guys go to jail, but justice is about more than punishment. Justice means different things in different situations, but at its core, justice is about fairness. People seek justice when they feel they have been treated unfairly in some way.

Everyone is different. People need different things to do their best. **Equality** doesn't mean everyone gets the same thing. It means everyone gets what they need in order to have the same opportunities. Some students have learning disabilities that make it difficult for them to read. It would be unfair to ask them to complete a test in the same amount of time as someone who is able to read faster. An equal system allows everyone the time they need to take the test. This ensures everyone is able to finish and is graded on their knowledge. This is a form of justice because it is fair to everyone.

Some groups of people, like students who struggle in school, may need more help to succeed. Giving them extra support is an example of justice.

BUILT TO EVOLVE

The Constitution of the United States forms the basis for our legal system. One of the most important parts of the US Constitution is its ability to change. New laws can be written. Old laws can be changed or entirely done away with. The Founding Fathers understood that they could not predict every law their new nation would need. Electric lights hadn't even been invented when the Constitution was written. It would have been impossible for the Founding Fathers to include laws to govern things like social media or driving. Having a flexible legal system allows laws to keep up with changing societies and technologies.

Having a legal system that can change also allows us to fix mistakes. Unfortunately, the legal system can be very slow to change. There was a time when women were not seen as equal to men. They were unable to vote or own property. Adult women were treated like children in the eyes of the law. It took women in the United States close to a hundred years of fighting to earn the right to vote. Whole

Economic Justice

People work in order to make money. In a fair system, everyone doing the same job would be paid the same. Unfortunately, this is not always the case. Women and people of color are regularly paid less than white men. This is known as a wage gap. Women and people of color are also less likely to be promoted to higher-paying positions. Closing these wage gaps is a form of economic justice.

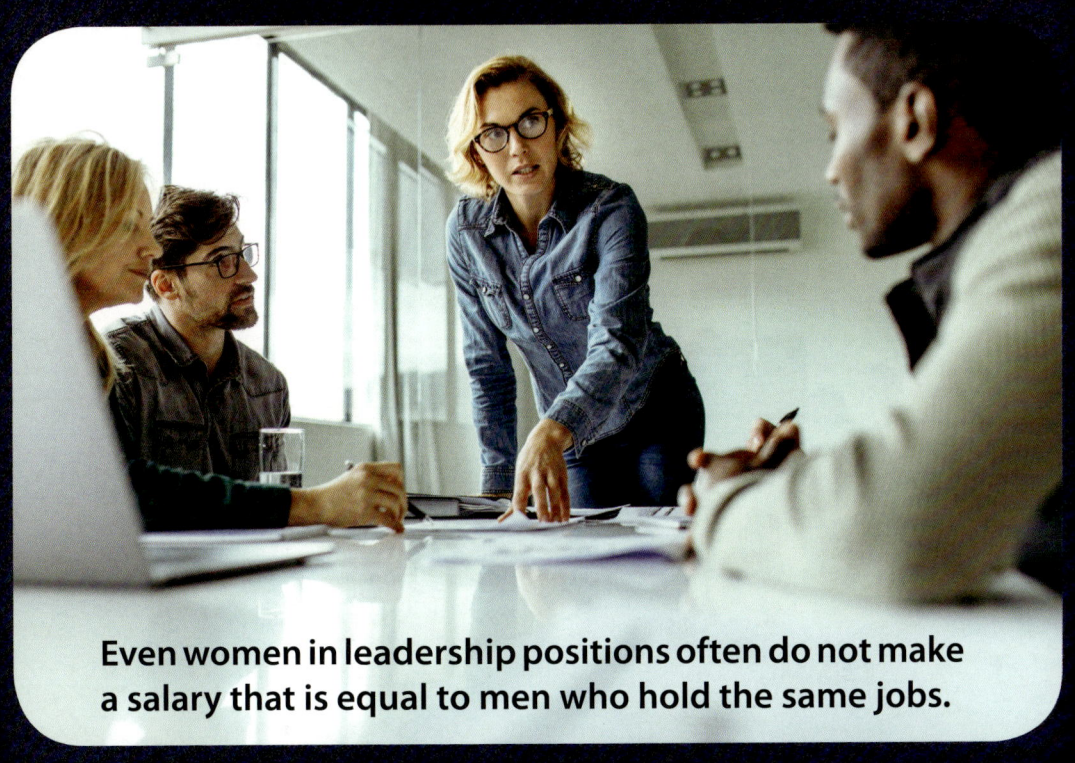

Even women in leadership positions often do not make a salary that is equal to men who hold the same jobs.

WHAT IS JUSTICE? 11

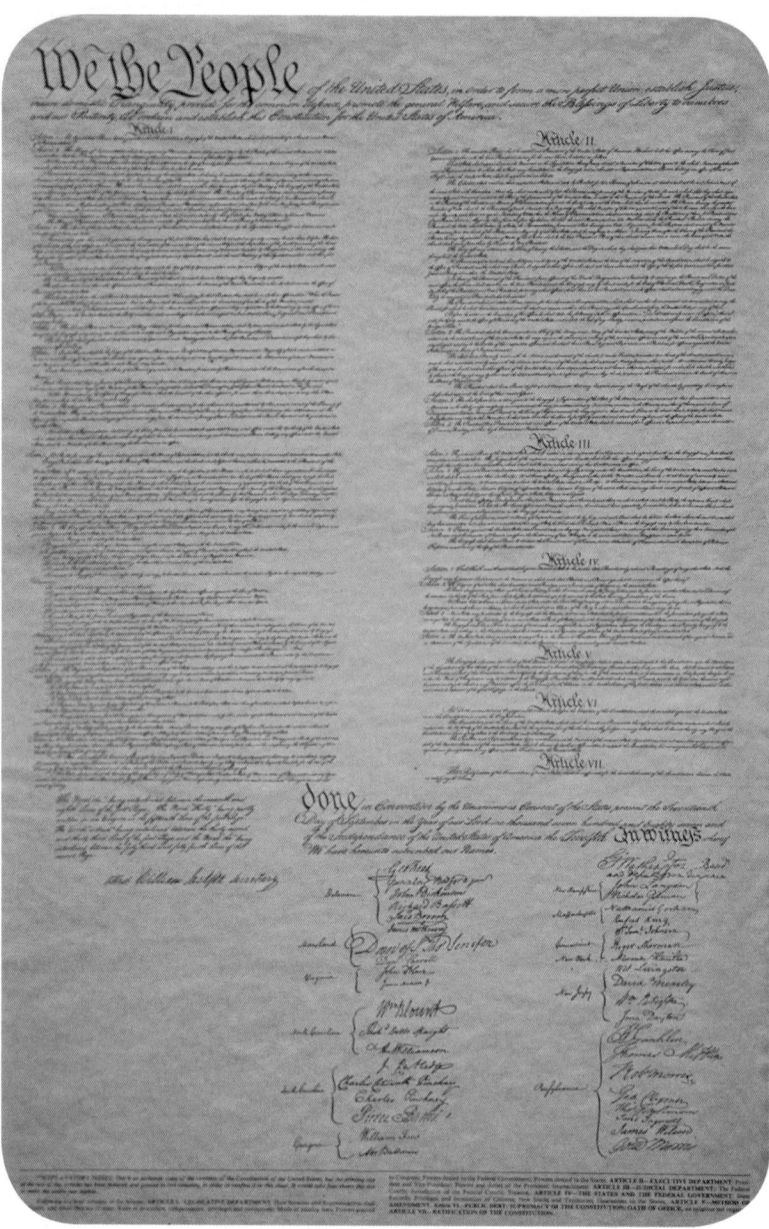

The Constitution is the basis of our legal system, and we often revisit it as new issues arise.

generations of women were denied justice before the legal system was changed. Even when women were officially granted the right to vote in 1920, it took even longer for women of color to be able to freely exercise their right to vote in the United States. It's important to remember that justice needs to include fair treatment for all.

two
Who Gets Justice?

Most laws are meant to keep people safe. Laws are written by politicians who have seen a need in their community. Most politicians have good intentions and want to write laws that will be good for everyone, but this doesn't always happen. The men who prevented women from voting thought they were doing what was best for everyone even though the law was unfair. While good laws can help protect people, bad laws can hurt people.

Systemic Oppression

Some laws have been used to prevent certain groups of people from having certain things or participating in some parts of society. This is called **systemic oppression**. Just because a system is legal doesn't

The US government tries to make laws that help and protect communities, but laws are not always fair.

mean it's fair to everyone. This is especially true for people of color—and black citizens in particular—who were granted equal rights many years after white Americans. The US system of government and laws was not specifically designed with these citizens in mind, and that has led to unfair treatment.

Redlining

Usually, when people buy property they get a loan called a mortgage from a bank. In the 1930s, the National Housing Act led to the creation of a system in the United States called "redlining." The Federal Housing Association drew colored lines around maps of neighborhoods in over two hundred cities. Residents of a neighborhood that had a red line would no longer be loaned money regardless of their income or ability to repay their loans. These redlined neighborhoods were usually made up of people of color. While this process was legal, it was unfair and oppressive to people of color. It continued until it was made illegal by the Fair Housing Act of 1968. This is an example of when a law was used to end systemic oppression.

FAIRNESS FOR PRISONERS

When a person breaks a law they may be forced to pay a fine or be sent to prison. If you misbehave at a party, you may be put in a timeout. During a timeout, you may be sent to another room and no longer allowed to take part in the fun. Prison is little like a "timeout" for adults. Many people think justice has

Some people believe that instead of just punishing inmates, prison should help them become better people.

been served when someone goes to prison. Some people think prison should be used to help prisoners become better people.

In some prisons, the goal is to help inmates understand why their actions were wrong and prepare them to do better in the future. This is known as **inmate reform**. Unfortunately, many prisons do not focus on making prisoners better people.

Many prisons are run by private companies. These companies make a profit from each prisoner. The prisons also earn money from prison labor. Prisoners do not have to be paid minimum wage. In the United States, prisoners make clothes and military gear and package many retail goods. Privately run prisons focus less on **rehabilitation** in favor of making a profit off prison labor. This process of using prisons to earn money for private companies is known as the prison industrial complex. Many activist groups believe it is a form of systemic oppression that targets people of color and the LGBTQ community.

Battling the Unconscious

three

Imagine that you have never seen a cat in real life. You've only seen cats on TV, where they are usually shown as dangerous predators with sharp claws. You may even know someone who has been scratched by a cat. When you finally meet someone's pet cat in real life you would probably be cautious around it even if you were told it was a very gentle cat.

This caution is caused by an unconscious bias, in this case against cats. Because you

Believing stereotypes can lead us to hold unfair and false ideas about people.

BATTLING THE UNCONSCIOUS   19

have mostly seen negative portrayals of cats you have unknowingly formed a bias that most cats are dangerous. This unconscious bias causes you to act differently than you otherwise would around someone's pet.

Everyone has unconscious biases. They affect how we feel and think about other people in ways we usually aren't aware of. These biases can make it hard for certain groups, like people of color, to be treated fairly, especially if they have been arrested and must face a trial.

A Fair Trial

The Constitution grants every American the right to be tried by a jury of their peers. A jury is a group of people who are asked to listen to the facts of a court case and decide if someone is innocent or guilty. Unconscious bias can make juries less likely to believe people who belong to certain racial, ethnic, or religious groups, which is unfair.

We can fight our unconscious biases by questioning why we believe the things we do. If you find that, like with the cat, your beliefs are based on

Racial Profiling

In the United States, black and white citizens commit about an equal number of drug-related crimes. However, black citizens are almost three times more likely to go to jail for drug-related crimes. This is because some police officers have unconscious biases that lead them to stop more people of color. When authority figures assume someone has done something based on their race, it's known as **racial profiling**. It is a form of oppression.

The #BlackLivesMatter movement has drawn attention to how black Americans have been victims of racial profiling and police violence.

what you see on TV, then you should do research to find out what the truth is.

It's also important to call out injustice when you see it. If you think someone is acting on their unconscious biases rather than fact, politely let them know. If you think someone is being treated unfairly

Because juries play an important role in deciding the outcomes of trials, they must try to look at the evidence without bias.

by a police officer, stay with that person. If you are able to use your cell phone, shoot a video of what happens. Filming the police is legal as long as you don't get in their way. It creates a clear record of what happened. It allows jurors to make decisions based on facts rather than what people say.

four
Working Toward Justice for All

When citizens become aware of injustice in their communities they can petition, or ask, the government to change the law. There are many ways to petition the government. You can write an email or send a letter. A phone call is an easy way to let your representative know what injustice you'd like corrected.

Citizens Respond to Unjust Laws

One powerful form of petition is known as a protest. When an oppressive law is passed, citizens often react by protesting. In 2017, President Donald Trump passed a travel ban that many people thought was oppressive to Muslim people. Citizens gathered at

President Donald Trump's attempt to ban travelers from countries with large Muslim populations sparked outrage among many American citizens.

Working Toward Justice for All

Rosa Parks practiced civil disobedience when she refused to give up her seat at the front of a bus to a white passenger.

airports immediately after the law was passed to show support for people who were no longer allowed to enter the country. The protest gave citizens an immediate way to show the government that they disagreed with the law. In a representative democracy like the United States, it's important for citizens to keep their representatives in government informed about their opinion.

When protests are not enough to get the attention of lawmakers some people practice **civil disobedience**. This is when a person intentionally

Restorative Justice

Our current justice system mainly focuses on punishing criminals. Supporting the needs of victims is not a part of the courts' job. Some prison-reform activists think it would be better if our justice system focused more on the needs and wants of the victim. **Restorative justice** allows people to say what they think would be a fair resolution to crimes they have been victims of. It's also more focused on making sure people get the help they need so they don't commit crimes in the future.

If we work together, welcoming all voices and treating everyone with respect, we can create a more just world.

breaks a law to show how unjust it is. A famous example of this is Rosa Parks, who in 1955 refused to give up her seat on a bus to a white man. Her arrest showed many people how unfair the law was. Civil disobedience is a powerful tool in the fight for justice. However, citizens who practice civil disobedience do risk being arrested and going to jail. When you see people practicing civil disobedience you should take it as an opportunity to learn more about an issue.

Fighting for Justice in Our Communities

Promoting justice is something everyone can do. One way to promote justice in your community is to volunteer at organizations that help the less fortunate.

Another important way to promote justice is to understand the laws of your community and how they affect all the different people of your community. When we understand the effect unconscious bias has on our legal system it is easier to spot unjust laws. You can promote justice by alerting your local politicians to laws you think do more harm than good.

The fight for justice will never be over. It is a living process that we can all take part in. Every time we do the right thing we make the world a more just place.

Words to Know

civil disobedience Peacefully breaking a law to show how unjust it is.
equality Making sure everyone gets what they need to succeed.
inmate reform Helping prisoners better themselves so they do not need to rely on criminal activity.
justice Fairness in behavior or treatment.
oppression Unfair treatment of a group of people by a ruling government.
racial profiling Assuming people are guilty of a crime based on their race or ethnicity.
rehabilitation The process of helping someone get better, either mentally or physically.
restorative justice A system of justice that focuses on the wants and needs of the victims of crime rather than just on punishing criminals.
systemic oppression When systems that should help people are unfair or oppressive to some.
unconscious Not fully aware; it can describe feelings and beliefs that we hold without realizing.

Learn More

Books

Linde, Barbara M. *Becoming a Supreme Court Justice*. New York, NY: Gareth Stevens, 2016.

McMeans, Julia. *Justice in Our Society*. New York, NY: Cavendish, 2018.

Ogden, Charlie. *Law & Justice*. New York, NY: Crabtree, 2017.

Websites

Kids Against Bullying
pacerkidsagainstbullying.org
This website inspires students to take action against bullying in their schools.

Race Project Kids
understandingrace.org/kids.html
Understand what it's like to walk in someone else's shoes at the Race Project.

Teaching Tolerance
splcenter.org/teaching-tolerance
Learn more about the fight to end discrimination.

Index

C
calling out injustice, 23
civil disobedience, 27–29
Constitution, 10, 21

E
economic justice, 11
equality, 4, 8–9, 10, 15

F
Fair Housing Act, 16
Founding Fathers, 10

G
government, 4, 15, 24, 27

I
inmate reform, 18

J
judicial branch, 4
juries, 5, 21–22, 23
justice, concept of, 4, 7, 8–9
"justice is blind," 5

L
laws, 4, 10, 14, 16
legal system, ability to change, 10–13

LGBTQ people, 6, 18

P
Parks, Rosa, 28
people of color, 6, 11, 13, 15, 16, 18, 21
petitioning the government, 24
police officers, 5, 21, 23
politicians, 14, 29
prisoners, 16–18
prison industrial complex, 18
prison labor, 18
protesting, 24–27
punishment, 4, 8, 27

R
racial profiling, 21
redlining, 16
research, doing, 22
restorative justice, 27

S
society, changes to, 6–7
systematic oppression, 14–15

T
Trump, Donald, 24

U
unconscious bias, 6, 19–21, 22, 29

V
voting rights, 10–13, 14

W
wage gap, 11
women, 10, 11–13, 14
working toward justice, 24–29